I0017416

IPHONE 15 FINAL SECRETS

What Apple Didn't Tell You About Their Game-Changing Features

A Year-Long Review and In-Depth Look at the Latest Innovations and Why They Matter

Alejandro S. Diego

Copyright © Alejandro S. Diego, 2024.

All rights reserved. No part of this publication may be reproduced, distributed, or transmitted in any form or by any means, including photocopying, recording, or other electronic or mechanical methods, without the prior written permission of the publisher, except in the case of brief quotations embodied in critical reviews and certain other noncommercial uses permitted by copyright law.

Table of Contents

Introduction

The iPhone 15 series, introduced with much fanfare nearly a year ago, marked a significant milestone in Apple's journey of innovation. As the tech world buzzed with anticipation, Apple unveiled a device that promised to revolutionize the smartphone experience once again. With its sleek titanium body, advanced camera system, and customizable action button, the iPhone 15 was poised to set new standards in the industry. But beyond the glossy presentations and marketing hype, what does this device truly offer?

In this book, we embark on a journey to uncover the real story behind the iPhone 15 Pro. Drawing from a year of extensive use and detailed analysis, we strip away the layers of polished advertising to reveal the genuine strengths and hidden weaknesses of this flagship phone. Our goal is to provide an honest, comprehensive review that goes beyond surface impressions, offering you the insights you need to make an informed decision.

As we delve into the core features of the iPhone 15 Pro, you'll discover the nuances that make it stand out in a crowded market. From the groundbreaking switch to a titanium frame, which redefines durability and elegance, to the powerful A17 chip that drives unparalleled performance, each aspect of the iPhone 15 Pro is scrutinized and evaluated. We'll explore the practical implications of its design choices, the real-world benefits of its advanced technologies, and the everyday experiences of users who have integrated this device into their lives.

Our exploration isn't just about the technical specs; it's about understanding how these innovations impact you, the user. Whether you're a tech enthusiast seeking the latest advancements or a casual user looking for a reliable companion, this book aims to bridge the gap between expectation and reality. We'll share personal anecdotes, user testimonials, and expert insights to paint a vivid picture of what living with the iPhone 15 Pro truly feels like.

In an era where smartphones have become indispensable tools, making the right choice can be daunting. This book serves as your guide, offering clarity and perspective in a landscape often clouded by marketing jargon. As we journey through the intricacies of the iPhone 15 Pro, you'll gain a deeper appreciation for its capabilities and limitations, empowering you to decide if it's the right fit for you.

Prepare to embark on an eye-opening adventure through the world of the iPhone 15 Pro. Whether you're here to confirm your purchase decision or simply satisfy your curiosity, this book promises to deliver an engaging and informative experience. So, turn the page, and let's dive into the fascinating realm of Apple's most talked-about smartphone, unveiling the secrets that lie beneath its sleek surface.

The Titanium Design

The transition from stainless steel to titanium in the iPhone 15 Pro is more than just a cosmetic change—it's a significant leap in materials science that redefines what users can expect from their smartphones. When Apple announced this shift, it was met with a mix of excitement and skepticism. After all, how much difference could a change in the phone's frame material really make? As it turns out, quite a bit.

Titanium, known for its exceptional strength-to-weight ratio, has long been a material of choice in industries where both durability and weight are critical factors—such as aerospace and high-performance sports equipment. By adopting titanium for the iPhone 15 Pro, Apple has not only reduced the phone's weight but also enhanced its overall resilience. The reduction in weight is immediately noticeable. When you hold the iPhone 15 Pro for the first time, there's a subtle but significant lightness that belies its robust build.

This isn't just a minor tweak; it's a fundamental improvement that enhances the phone's portability without compromising its structural integrity.

Durability is another area where titanium excels. Unlike stainless steel, which can show scratches and dings over time, titanium is more resistant to the wear and tear of daily use. This means your iPhone 15 Pro is more likely to maintain its pristine appearance, even after months or years of use. It's a phone designed not just to look good out of the box, but to stay looking good for as long as you own it.

The user experience is also significantly enhanced by this transition. The lighter weight makes the iPhone 15 Pro more comfortable to hold for extended periods, whether you're reading, gaming, or browsing. It's less likely to cause the fatigue that can come with heavier devices, making it a more pleasant companion for daily activities. Additionally, the enhanced durability means you can be less worried about accidental drops or knocks. This peace of mind allows you to use the phone more freely and confidently, knowing that it's built to withstand the rigors of everyday life.

Moreover, the aesthetic appeal of titanium cannot be overlooked. It has a unique luster and feel that sets it apart from other materials. The finish is sleek and sophisticated, giving the iPhone 15 Pro a premium look and feel that matches its high-end capabilities. This combination of beauty and brawn is a hallmark of Apple's design philosophy, and the iPhone 15 Pro embodies it perfectly.

In practical terms, the shift to titanium also means better heat dissipation. Titanium conducts heat differently than stainless steel, which can lead to better performance during intensive tasks. Whether you're playing graphically demanding games, editing high-resolution videos, or running multiple apps simultaneously, the iPhone 15 Pro stays cooler, which helps maintain optimal performance.

In summary, the transition from stainless steel to titanium in the iPhone 15 Pro is a game-changer. It improves the device's weight, durability, user comfort, and aesthetic appeal, while also contributing to better performance under heavy use. This thoughtful and impactful design choice underscores Apple's commitment to continuous improvement and innovation, ensuring that the iPhone 15 Pro is not just a step forward, but a leap into a more refined and capable future.

Display Sizes and Future Prospects

The iPhone 15 Pro series offers display sizes that cater to a wide range of user preferences. The iPhone 15 Pro features a 6.1-inch display, while the iPhone 15 Pro Max boasts a larger 6.7-inch display. These sizes have become somewhat standard in the industry, providing a balanced mix of usability and immersive viewing experiences. For many users, these dimensions hit a sweet spot, offering enough screen real estate for multimedia consumption, gaming, and productivity without making the device cumbersome to handle.

The 6.1-inch display on the iPhone 15 Pro is perfect for those who prefer a more compact device. It's easy to operate with one hand, fits comfortably in pockets and small bags, and is ideal for users who prioritize portability without sacrificing performance or display quality. On the other hand, the 6.7-inch display of the iPhone 15 Pro Max is tailored for users who enjoy larger screens for watching videos, reading, and gaming. The larger screen size provides a more immersive experience, making it a popular choice among media enthusiasts and gamers.

Looking ahead to the iPhone 16 series, there are strong indications that Apple will be increasing the display sizes even further. Rumors suggest that the iPhone 16 Pro models will feature a 6.3-inch display for the Pro and a massive 6.9-inch display for the Pro Max. This shift reflects an ongoing trend towards larger screens, driven by consumer demand for more immersive viewing experiences and enhanced productivity capabilities.

The anticipated increase in display size raises interesting questions about user preferences and ergonomics. For many users, the current 6.1 and 6.7-inch displays are already at the upper limits of what is comfortable to use one-handed. The move to 6.3 and 6.9 inches could push these limits further, potentially requiring users to adapt to new ways of interacting with their devices. Features like reachability mode and enhanced gesture controls will become increasingly important to maintain usability on these larger screens.

The decision to increase display sizes is likely driven by several factors. Larger screens provide more space for multitasking, which is increasingly important as smartphones become central to our work and personal lives. They also enhance the experience of consuming media, playing games, and using augmented reality applications. For Apple, it's about staying ahead in a competitive market where screen size and quality are key differentiators.

However, it's essential to recognize that not all users prefer larger screens. Many still value the convenience and ease of use that comes with smaller devices. Apple's challenge will be to balance these varying preferences, possibly by offering a range of sizes within the Pro lineup or enhancing features that improve the usability of larger screens.

In summary, the current display sizes of the iPhone 15 Pro and Pro Max strike a balance between usability and immersive experience, catering to different user needs. The anticipated changes in the iPhone 16 series reflect a trend towards even larger screens, promising enhanced productivity and media consumption experiences. As the market evolves, Apple's ability to innovate in both hardware and software will be crucial in meeting the diverse preferences of its user base, ensuring that each new iteration of the iPhone continues to set the standard in smartphone design and functionality.

The Revolutionary Action Button

The introduction of the action button in the iPhone 15 Pro series marks a significant departure from the traditional design, replacing the long-standing ring/silent switch with a more versatile and customizable control. This innovative feature offers users unprecedented flexibility in configuring their iPhones to better suit their individual needs and preferences. The action button, capable of being programmed to perform a wide range of tasks, has quickly become one of the standout features of the iPhone 15 Pro.

Customization options for the action button are extensive. Users can assign it to perform simple tasks such as toggling between ring and silent modes, launching the camera, turning on the flashlight, or activating Do Not Disturb. But the possibilities don't stop there. With the integration of Apple's Shortcuts app, the action button can be customized to trigger complex sequences of actions, effectively turning it into a powerful productivity tool. This level of customization allows users to tailor their iPhones to fit their unique workflows and routines, making the device more personal and efficient.

In real-life applications, the action button has proven to be incredibly useful. For instance, some users have programmed it to open specific apps they frequently use, such as their messaging app or a navigation app. Others have set it to activate voice memos for quick note-taking on the go. The action button's ability to quickly call a pre-set contact has been a favorite feature for many, especially those who need to stay in touch with family or colleagues at the press of a button. One user shared how they use the action button to call their spouse directly, making it an invaluable feature during their daily commute.

The versatility of the action button extends beyond just personal use. It has significant implications for accessibility, providing users with motor impairments a more convenient way to interact with their iPhones. By customizing the button to perform essential functions, these users can navigate their devices more easily and efficiently, enhancing their overall user experience.

However, despite its many advantages, the action button also presents some potential for improvement. One of the main criticisms is its limited range of input methods. Currently, the button supports only a single press-and-hold action. Users have expressed a desire for more versatility, such as the ability to double-tap, triple-tap, or distinguish between short and long presses to trigger different functions. This enhancement could significantly increase the button's utility, allowing for even more customization and functionality.

Another missed opportunity lies in the lack of integration with third-party apps. While the Shortcuts app provides a workaround, direct support from popular third-party apps could streamline the user experience and expand the button's potential uses. For example, integrating with fitness apps to start and stop workouts or with smart home apps to control connected devices could further enhance the appeal of the action button.

Despite these areas for improvement, the action button represents a significant step forward in smartphone design. It embodies Apple's commitment to innovation and user-centric design, offering a feature that truly adapts to the needs and preferences of its users. As the technology evolves, it is likely that future iterations will address these limitations, unlocking even greater potential for this revolutionary feature.

The action button on the iPhone 15 Pro is a testament to how thoughtful design can enhance user experience, making everyday interactions with technology more intuitive and efficient. It stands as a prime example of how Apple continues to push the boundaries of what a smartphone can do, ensuring that its devices not only meet but exceed user expectations.

Performance Powered by A17 Chip

The performance of the iPhone 15 Pro is undeniably one of its most impressive aspects, largely due to the power of the A17 chip. This next-generation processor marks a significant leap forward in both speed and efficiency, setting a new benchmark for what users can expect from a smartphone. When comparing the A17 chip to its predecessors in the iPhone 13 and 14 models, the advancements become clear, offering a glimpse into the future of mobile technology.

The A17 chip is built on a cutting-edge 5-nanometer process, which allows for more transistors in the same space, resulting in greater power efficiency and performance. This translates into a noticeable boost in speed and responsiveness. Tasks that might have taken a second or two on previous models are executed almost instantaneously on the iPhone 15 Pro. Whether it's launching apps, multitasking, or processing complex graphics, the A17 chip handles everything with remarkable ease.

When comparing the iPhone 15 Pro to the iPhone 13 and 14, the differences in performance are striking. The A15 and A16 chips in the iPhone 13 and 14 were already powerful, but the A17 takes things to a whole new level. Benchmarks show that the A17 chip offers up to a 20% increase in processing speed and a similar improvement in graphics performance. This means that not only does the iPhone 15 Pro perform everyday tasks faster, but it also excels in more demanding applications, such as video editing, 3D rendering, and gaming.

In real-world usage, these improvements are more than just numbers on a page. The efficiency and speed of the A17 chip translate into a smoother, more responsive user experience. Apps open and close seamlessly, and multitasking feels more fluid than ever. This is particularly noticeable in intensive applications, where the iPhone 15 Pro maintains its performance without overheating or draining the battery quickly. Users have reported that even after hours of gaming or video streaming, the device remains cool and continues to perform optimally.

Battery life is another area where the A17 chip shines. Its efficiency allows the iPhone 15 Pro to manage power consumption more effectively, extending battery life compared to previous models. This means users can go longer between charges, even with heavy use. Whether you're navigating a busy workday, traveling, or enjoying a weekend of leisure, the improved battery performance ensures that the iPhone 15 Pro keeps up with your lifestyle.

The overall impact of the A17 chip on the user experience is profound. It enhances every interaction with the device, making it feel more responsive and capable. Users transitioning from older models will immediately notice the difference in speed and efficiency. The improved performance also ensures that the iPhone 15 Pro remains future-proof, capable of handling new software updates and applications that may demand more processing power.

Moreover, the A17 chip's capabilities extend beyond performance. Its advanced neural engine enhances machine learning tasks, enabling features like improved photo and video processing, more accurate voice recognition, and advanced augmented reality experiences. This makes the iPhone 15 Pro not just a powerful tool, but an intelligent one that adapts to your needs.

In conclusion, the A17 chip in the iPhone 15 Pro represents a significant advancement in smartphone technology. Its superior performance compared to the A15 and A16 chips in previous models, coupled with its efficiency and real-world benefits, makes it a game-changer. The enhanced speed, battery life, and overall user experience solidify the iPhone 15 Pro's position as a leader in the market, showcasing Apple's commitment to pushing the boundaries of innovation and delivering unparalleled quality to its users.

Battery Life: Expectations vs. Reality

Battery life has always been a crucial aspect of any smartphone, and the iPhone 15 Pro is no exception. With each new model, Apple aims to enhance the battery performance, promising longer usage times and more efficient power management. However, the real-world performance of a battery can often differ from initial expectations. Let's explore the battery life of the iPhone 15 Pro, analyzing its performance over time, comparing it with previous models, and offering practical tips for maximizing battery longevity.

When the iPhone 15 Pro was launched, Apple touted significant improvements in battery life, thanks to the new A17 chip and more efficient power management systems. Users were excited about the prospect of a phone that could easily last through a busy day of use without needing a recharge. Initial tests supported these claims, showing that the iPhone 15 Pro could handle heavy use, including streaming video, playing games, and running multiple apps simultaneously, without rapidly depleting the battery.

However, battery performance can change over time as the device is subjected to daily wear and tear. After nearly a year of use, many iPhone 15 Pro owners have reported on the device's battery health. On average, users have seen the battery health stabilize around 90-92%, which is a decent retention rate. This suggests that the battery degradation is relatively slow, maintaining its performance longer compared to previous models like the iPhone 14 Pro, which saw more significant drops in battery health within the same timeframe.

Comparing the iPhone 15 Pro to its predecessors, the improvements are clear. The iPhone 14 Pro, while powerful, suffered from more noticeable battery degradation and shorter battery life under similar usage patterns. The iPhone 13 Pro, with its A15 chip, also lagged behind in terms of both initial battery performance and long-term durability. The efficiency of the A17 chip in the iPhone 15 Pro, combined with optimized software, results in better overall battery management.

One of the significant factors contributing to the iPhone 15 Pro's better battery performance is its ability to manage background processes more effectively. The A17 chip allows for more intelligent allocation of resources, ensuring that battery-draining tasks do not unnecessarily consume power. This means that users can enjoy smoother performance without worrying as much about rapid battery drain.

Despite these advancements, there are always ways to further maximize your iPhone 15 Pro's battery life. Here are some practical tips:

1. **Optimize Settings**: Adjusting settings like screen brightness, enabling auto-brightness, and reducing the time before the screen locks can significantly save battery life.
2. **Manage Background Activities**: Limit background app refresh for apps that do not

need constant updates. This can be done through the Settings app, under General > Background App Refresh.

3. **Use Low Power Mode**: Activating Low Power Mode when your battery is running low can extend usage time by reducing power consumption. This mode can be enabled through Settings or via the Control Center.

4. **Update iOS Regularly**: Apple frequently releases updates that include optimizations for battery performance. Keeping your iPhone up to date ensures you benefit from these improvements.

5. **Monitor Battery Usage**: The Battery section in the Settings app provides insights into which apps are consuming the most power. Identifying and managing these apps can help improve battery life.

6. **Avoid Extreme Temperatures**: Both high and low temperatures can negatively affect battery health. Try to avoid exposing your iPhone to extreme conditions.

7. **Use Optimized Battery Charging**: This feature, found in the Battery Health section of Settings, slows down battery aging by learning your charging routine and waiting to finish charging past 80% until you need to use it.

By following these tips, you can ensure that your iPhone 15 Pro remains efficient and reliable throughout its lifespan. While the iPhone 15 Pro already offers improved battery performance compared to previous models, proactive management and good charging habits can make a significant difference in maintaining its health over time.

In conclusion, the iPhone 15 Pro's battery life generally meets and often exceeds expectations, thanks to the advanced A17 chip and efficient power management. While some battery degradation over time is inevitable, the device performs admirably, especially when compared to earlier models. By implementing smart usage practices, users can maximize their battery life, ensuring their iPhone 15

Pro remains a powerful and dependable companion for years to come.

Mobile Gaming: A New Frontier?

Apple has long positioned the iPhone as not just a communication device but a powerful mobile gaming platform. With the iPhone 15 Pro, the company has made bold claims about its capabilities, touting the A17 chip's prowess in handling graphically intensive games and delivering a console-like gaming experience. But how does this stand up to real-world use, and how does the iPhone 15 Pro compare to dedicated gaming devices?

Apple's marketing highlights the iPhone 15 Pro as the ultimate mobile gaming machine. The A17 chip, with its advanced GPU and enhanced processing power, is said to offer smooth gameplay, fast load times, and stunning graphics. The high-refresh-rate display, combined with HDR support, aims to provide an immersive visual experience, making games look vibrant and lifelike. Additionally, the extensive library of games available on the App

Store, from casual titles to AAA games, positions the iPhone 15 Pro as a versatile gaming platform.

However, user experiences provide a more nuanced view of these claims. Many users appreciate the iPhone 15 Pro's ability to handle demanding games with ease. Popular titles like Genshin Impact, Call of Duty Mobile, and Fortnite run smoothly, with minimal lag and excellent graphics quality. The responsive touchscreen and high-refresh-rate display enhance gameplay, making controls more intuitive and visuals more fluid.

Moreover, the convenience of having a powerful gaming device that fits in your pocket cannot be overstated. Mobile gaming on the iPhone 15 Pro allows users to play anywhere, anytime, without the need for additional hardware. This portability is a significant advantage over traditional gaming consoles, which are typically confined to the living room.

Despite these strengths, there are practical limitations to consider. Extended gaming sessions can lead to the device heating up, which can impact performance and comfort. While the A17 chip is efficient, the compact design of a smartphone means that it cannot dissipate heat as effectively as larger gaming consoles or PCs. Battery life is another concern; intensive gaming can drain the battery quickly, necessitating frequent recharges or use while plugged in, which can be cumbersome.

When comparing the iPhone 15 Pro to dedicated gaming devices like the Nintendo Switch, Steam Deck, or even traditional gaming consoles, several differences emerge. Dedicated gaming devices are designed with gaming as their primary function, often featuring physical controls, larger screens, and superior cooling systems. These elements contribute to a more immersive and comfortable gaming experience over extended periods.

The Nintendo Switch, for example, offers physical buttons and joysticks, which many gamers prefer for precision control in action-packed games. Its hybrid design allows for both handheld and docked play, providing flexibility that the iPhone 15 Pro cannot match. The Steam Deck, with its powerful hardware and access to the vast library of PC games, offers a gaming experience closer to a high-end gaming PC than a smartphone can provide.

However, the iPhone 15 Pro excels in its versatility and ecosystem integration. It's not just a gaming device but also a powerful smartphone with a vast array of functionalities. The App Store's extensive game library includes many titles not available on other platforms, and the seamless integration with other Apple services enhances the overall user experience. For casual gamers or those looking for convenience and portability, the iPhone 15 Pro is an excellent choice.

In summary, while the iPhone 15 Pro may not fully replace dedicated gaming devices for hardcore gamers, it offers a compelling mobile gaming experience. Apple's claims about the A17 chip's capabilities hold up well in real-world use, providing smooth and visually impressive gameplay. The convenience of having a powerful gaming device in your pocket is unmatched, though there are practical limitations like heat management and battery life to consider. Ultimately, the iPhone 15 Pro stands out as a versatile and capable device that brings high-quality gaming to the mobile realm, bridging the gap between casual and serious gaming in a way that few other devices can.

The Pro Camera System

The five-times telephoto zoom lens in the iPhone 15 Pro Max represents a significant leap forward in smartphone camera technology. Apple has consistently pushed the boundaries of what a phone camera can achieve, and with this lens, they have introduced a feature that not only enhances photography but also expands the creative possibilities for users. This advanced lens allows for greater versatility in capturing distant subjects with clarity and precision, making it a standout feature of the iPhone 15 Pro Max.

The practical uses of the five-times telephoto zoom lens are vast and varied. For many users, it fundamentally changes how they approach photography and videography. Whether capturing a stunning landscape, snapping a candid shot at a social event, or documenting a child's sports game, the ability to zoom in without losing detail is invaluable. The lens brings distant subjects into sharp focus, producing images with rich detail and minimal noise.

One notable application of the telephoto lens is in wildlife photography. Enthusiasts can now capture close-up shots of animals in their natural habitat without disturbing them. This capability is particularly beneficial for bird watchers, who often need to photograph subjects from a distance. The clarity and detail achievable with the five-times zoom lens rival that of standalone cameras, making the iPhone 15 Pro Max a powerful tool for nature photography.

Portrait photography also benefits significantly from the telephoto lens. The ability to zoom in allows photographers to create a more intimate and focused composition, isolating the subject from the background and creating a beautiful bokeh effect. This feature enhances the quality of portrait shots, giving them a professional look that was previously difficult to achieve with a smartphone camera.

User experiences with the telephoto lens have been overwhelmingly positive. Many have praised its performance in various lighting conditions, noting that it maintains sharpness and color accuracy even in low light. The seamless transition between the standard wide-angle lens and the telephoto lens allows for a smooth shooting experience, making it easy to switch perspectives without missing a moment. Users have also appreciated the ability to capture high-quality photos and videos at events like concerts and sports games, where getting close to the action is often not possible.

Another groundbreaking feature of the iPhone 15 Pro Max is its ability to record spatial video. This new dimension of video recording leverages the advanced capabilities of the camera system to capture depth and spatial information, creating a more immersive viewing experience. Spatial video recording uses multiple lenses to gather data on the distance and positioning of objects in the frame, which can then be played back in a way that simulates a three-dimensional environment.

The implications of spatial video are profound, especially with the growing interest in augmented reality (AR) and virtual reality (VR). For content creators, this feature opens up new avenues for storytelling and engagement. Imagine watching a travel vlog where you can feel as though you are walking through the streets of a foreign city or experiencing a concert with a sense of depth that makes it feel like you are in the front row. Spatial video enhances the realism and immersion of recorded content, making it more engaging and impactful.

For everyday users, spatial video offers an exciting way to capture and relive personal moments. Family gatherings, vacations, and special events can be recorded with a level of detail and immersion that traditional video cannot match. When played back on compatible devices, these recordings provide a richer and more dynamic viewing experience, bringing memories to life in a new and exciting way.

In conclusion, the five-times telephoto zoom lens and the ability to record spatial video are two standout features of the iPhone 15 Pro Max that elevate it above previous models. The telephoto lens offers practical benefits for various photography needs, from wildlife and portrait photography to capturing events and everyday moments with greater clarity and detail. Spatial video recording introduces a new dimension to video content, enhancing the immersive experience for both creators and viewers. Together, these features underscore Apple's commitment to pushing the boundaries of smartphone technology and providing users with innovative tools to capture and share their world.

Pricing and Value Proposition

Apple's pricing strategy for the iPhone 15 Pro series is both a reflection of the premium features it offers and a careful balance to maintain its competitive edge in the high-end smartphone market. With the base model of the iPhone 15 Pro starting at $999 and the iPhone 15 Pro Max starting at $1,099, Apple has positioned these devices as top-tier products that justify their price through cutting-edge technology and superior build quality. The pricing also includes more storage options at the base level, providing users with better value right from the start.

Analyzing the cost of the iPhone 15 Pro involves looking beyond the sticker price to understand the value it brings in terms of features, performance, and longevity. The device boasts a plethora of advancements, such as the titanium frame, A17 chip, five-times telephoto zoom lens, and the revolutionary action button, all of which contribute to its high cost. These features are designed to enhance the user experience, making the iPhone 15 Pro not just a phone, but a powerful tool for communication, productivity, and entertainment.

When comparing the iPhone 15 Pro to its predecessors and competitors, the value proposition becomes clearer. The transition to titanium not only improves durability but also reduces weight, making the device more comfortable to use over long periods. The A17 chip ensures that the phone can handle the most demanding tasks with ease, from gaming to video editing, providing a seamless and lag-free experience. The camera system, particularly the telephoto zoom lens, sets a new standard for smartphone photography, offering capabilities that rival even dedicated cameras.

For users considering whether to upgrade, the decision hinges on a few key factors. If you currently own an iPhone 13 or older model, the jump to the iPhone 15 Pro represents a significant upgrade in terms of performance, camera quality, and overall user experience. The A17 chip alone offers a substantial boost in speed and efficiency, making everyday tasks smoother and more enjoyable. Additionally, the new features like the action button and spatial video recording provide unique functionalities that enhance the versatility of the device.

For those with an iPhone 14, the choice to upgrade may be more nuanced. While the improvements in the iPhone 15 Pro are notable, they may not be essential for all users. If your current device meets your needs and you are satisfied with its performance, waiting for the next generation might be a prudent choice. However, if you are a heavy user who demands the latest technology and the best possible performance, the iPhone 15 Pro offers enough enhancements to justify the upgrade.

In terms of value for money, the iPhone 15 Pro stands out in several areas. The build quality and materials used ensure that the device will last longer and withstand the rigors of daily use better than many competitors. The performance improvements translate into better efficiency, which can extend the usable life of the phone. Additionally, Apple's ecosystem, including software updates and customer support, adds significant value, ensuring that your investment remains relevant and functional for years to come.

For those on the fence about purchasing the iPhone 15 Pro, considering refurbished models or waiting for seasonal discounts could provide a more cost-effective way to obtain this high-end device. Apple's refurbished products come with a warranty and are often indistinguishable from new devices, offering substantial savings. Alternatively, purchasing the iPhone 15 Pro through carrier deals or trade-in programs can reduce the upfront cost, making it more accessible.

Ultimately, whether the iPhone 15 Pro is worth the upgrade depends on your specific needs and how much you value the latest advancements in technology. For tech enthusiasts, professionals who rely on their phone for demanding tasks, or anyone looking to future-proof their device, the iPhone 15 Pro offers a compelling package that justifies its premium price. For more casual users or those content with their current device, the decision may come down to personal preference and budget considerations.

In summary, Apple's pricing strategy for the iPhone 15 Pro reflects its position as a premium product packed with advanced features and superior performance. While the cost is high, the value it offers in terms of durability, functionality, and user experience makes it a worthwhile investment for those seeking the best in smartphone technology. Whether you choose to upgrade now or wait for future models, the iPhone 15 Pro sets a new standard in the smartphone market, delivering a blend of innovation and excellence that is hard to match.

Conclusion

The journey through the iPhone 15 Pro Max's features and performance reveals a device that stands at the pinnacle of smartphone technology. Throughout this exploration, we have dissected the key aspects that make the iPhone 15 Pro Max a remarkable piece of technology, from its innovative titanium design and the revolutionary action button to the powerhouse A17 chip and the advanced five-times telephoto zoom lens. These features collectively elevate the user experience, offering improvements in durability, performance, and versatility.

One of the standout innovations is the transition to a titanium frame, which not only enhances the device's durability but also reduces its weight, making it more comfortable to use over extended periods. This change, though subtle at first glance, significantly impacts the daily usability and longevity of the phone. The introduction of the action button adds a new level of customization, allowing users to tailor their device to better fit their unique workflows and preferences. This feature alone exemplifies Apple's commitment to user-centric design.

The A17 chip is another milestone, delivering exceptional speed and efficiency that sets a new benchmark for mobile processors. This advancement ensures that the iPhone 15 Pro Max handles everything from intensive gaming to professional-grade video editing with ease, maintaining smooth performance and long battery life. Coupled with this is the five-times telephoto zoom lens, which brings professional-level photography capabilities to a smartphone, allowing users to capture stunning detail and clarity from a distance.

Additionally, the ability to record spatial video introduces a new dimension to video content creation, enhancing the immersive quality of recordings and opening up new possibilities for augmented reality applications. These features collectively underscore Apple's innovative spirit and its pursuit of excellence in every aspect of smartphone design.

As we conclude, it is clear that the iPhone 15 Pro Max is more than just an incremental upgrade; it is a significant leap forward in multiple areas. For potential buyers, several considerations can guide your decision. If you currently own an older model, particularly anything before the iPhone 13, the iPhone 15 Pro Max offers substantial upgrades that justify the investment. The enhanced performance, superior camera capabilities, and advanced features like the action button and spatial video recording make it a compelling choice.

For those with an iPhone 14, the decision to upgrade may hinge on how much you value the specific improvements offered by the iPhone 15 Pro Max. If you are someone who regularly pushes your device to its limits with demanding applications and values having the latest technology, the upgrade is likely worth it. However, if your current device meets your needs and you are content with its performance, waiting for the next iteration might be a more prudent option.

In terms of value for money, the iPhone 15 Pro Max stands strong. The build quality, backed by the durability of the titanium frame and the long-term performance of the A17 chip, ensures that your investment is well-protected. Moreover, Apple's commitment to software updates and support means your device will remain current and functional for years to come, further enhancing its value proposition.

For those seeking to maximize their investment, considering options like refurbished models, carrier deals, or trade-in programs can provide significant savings without sacrificing quality. These options make the iPhone 15 Pro Max more accessible while still delivering the same top-tier experience.

In conclusion, the iPhone 15 Pro Max is a testament to Apple's ability to innovate and push the boundaries of what a smartphone can achieve. It brings together a blend of cutting-edge technology, thoughtful design, and user-focused features that set it apart in the crowded smartphone market. Whether you are a tech enthusiast, a professional seeking the best tools for your work, or a casual user looking for a reliable and powerful device, the iPhone 15 Pro Max offers something for everyone. It is a device that not only meets but exceeds expectations, promising to enhance your digital life in myriad ways.

www.ingramcontent.com/pod-product-compliance
Lightning Source LLC
LaVergne TN
LVHW051624050326
832903LV00033B/4641